Original Title: Intimate Elixirs



Editors: Theodor Taimla
Autor: Melani Helimets
ISBN 978-9916-39-447-2

# Intimate Elixirs

*Melani Helimets*

**Togetherness Tea**

Brew a pot of warmth and cheer,
For those we hold so very near.
Steam arising, hearts entwine,
In the dance of the togetherness vine.

Sips of solace, sips of grace,
The room alight with each embraced.
Laughter spills, a soothing sea,
Cups clink in harmony,

Through the steam, our stories weave,
A tapestry that love conceives.
In every drop, affection grows,
Togetherness tea, our hearts propose.

Let us linger, let us stay,
In the comfort of this shared array.
Friendship's flavor, bold and free,
In the sacred brew of togetherness tea.

## Euphoria's Essence Extract

Whispers of bliss, in the vials of night,
Captured in essence, a luminous flight.
Droplets of joy, so pure, so intact,
Spirits soar high on this euphoric extract.

Aroma of rapture, the essence permeates,
Through every sense, euphoria radiates.
Hearts pulse quicker, eyes glint with delight,
In this concoction, stars seem more bright.

Behold the elixir, in a dance with fate,
It swirls with the promise to animate.
Laughter imbued in this potion's effect,
The spirit's own symphony, for souls to reflect.

In the essence of euphoria, we lightly tread,
Through fields of ecstasy, joyously spread.
With each sip, a paradise unveiled,
In the magic of the essence, we're lovingly held.

## Enthralled by Essence

Gentle whispers of the jasmine breeze,
Entwining souls in tender tease,
Nature's breath doth softly quell,
The restless hearts it doth compel.

Underneath the moon's pale light,
Enthralled essence dances in the night,
Stars above in wonder gaze,
At the earthly spirits' silent praise.

Velvet petals in dusk's embrace,
Sweep across the tranquil space,
Serenity's song through leaves does roam,
As essence enthralls and beckons home.

## Desire's Decanted Dream

In vials of night, dreams poured anew,
The silhouettes of desire grew,
Each drop a wish, a hope, a scream,
Distilling softly in the stream.

A decanter holding passion's wine,
Swirling with the sands of time,
Aged in the cask of fervent hearts,
Where every longing plays its parts.

The pour is smooth, the scent is rich,
A tapestry of feelings stitch,
Desire's decanted dream alight,
The embers of the soul take flight.

## Sensations of the Subtle Sapor

A whisper of taste upon the air,
Delicate, faint, and oh so rare,
Each flavor a note, a subtle hue,
Sensations of sapor breaking through.

A fusion of spice, a touch of sweet,
A culinary anthem, complete,
Savory secrets of zest unfold,
A symphony of tastes, brave and bold.

In every morsel, a story told,
Of cultures, climates, young and old,
A journey through a world untapped,
Where sapor's subtleties are mapped.

## Caresses in a Cup

Steam rises in the fragile light,
Heralding the sun's first sight,
Warmth that blooms from deep within,
Soft caresses in a cup begin.

A blend of beans, earth's offering,
Black elixir, morning's king,
Each sip, a touch, a gentle hug,
Wrapped in the comfort, cozy and smug.

The dance of flavors on the tongue,
A song of awakening unsung,
Tranquil moments, the day's soft prep,
In this tender, liquid caress.

## Sympathy's Sweetened Spirits

In gentle whispers, sympathy speaks,
A tender touch to the one who's weak.
It mends the heart with its sweetened balm,
Calming the mind like a soothing psalm.

Across the silence, kind words flow,
A stream of love that begins to glow.
With every gesture, warmth is instilled,
In spaces of sorrow, emptiness filled.

Shared pains embraced in the softest hold,
Sympathy's spirit is pure like gold.
Knitting the threads of solace spun,
Till darkness fades to the morning sun.

## Mutual Muse Mix

Two souls entwined in creative dance,
Ideas merge in a mutual glance.
Each thought a spark, together they fuse,
Forging a bond, the mutual muse.

Your words, my canvas, our palette blends,
The art of kinship that never ends.
Sculpting our dreams with harmonious mix,
On the canvas of time, brushstrokes fix.

Rhythms converge in a symphony,
Composing life's shared epiphany.
With each verse penned, our story grows,
In literary love, the mutual muse shows.

## Captivation's Caring Concoction

With a drop of joy, a pinch of grace,
A potion brewed in the heart's embrace.
Captivation swells in caring eyes,
Concocting bonds that empathize.

In the cauldron of compassion's might,
Bubble feelings of pure delight.
Gentle hands stir in sweet affection,
Whispers of care, a mirrored reflection.

Elixir of empathy, rare to find,
A dose of kindness, for ties that bind.
The mixture's ready with a loving touch,
Healing hearts in its caring clutch.

## Enchantment's Elixir

Brewed with whispers of the mystic moon,
Enchantment's elixir will be ready soon.
The drink of dreams, from star's soft shimmer,
In every sip, the night's glimmer.

A chalice filled with twilight's essence,
Glowing with fairytales' luminescence.
Sipping slowly, the potion sways,
Through tales of old and bygone days.

Intoxicated by the magic poured,
Reality's grip is briefly ignored.
In each draught, the world beguiles,
Elixir of enchantment, bewitch and smiles.

## Ardor's Artful Aperitif

In the palette of dusk, our passions pour,
As twilight whispers through the open door.
Canvas of stars betwixt our fervent sighs,
In the hush of evening, our ardor lies.

With a touch as tender as the night's embrace,
Our silhouettes entwine in dance, with grace.
Each heartbeat an artist, bold and devout,
Painting desire on the canvass of doubt.

From lips, a sip of whispered, yearning need,
In the muted eve, our inhibitions freed.
Eyes alight with fireflies' enchanting light,
Savoring love's aperitif in the night.

## Interlace's Intoxicating Infusion

Threads of destiny, intwined and fraught,
Seamlessly stitched with the dreams we've caught.
Interlacing fingers, a tapestry spun,
In the loom of minutes, our souls are one.

The potion of promises, silently shared,
In intertwined whispers, lives are bared.
Spiraling hopes with tendrils that twine,
In the infusion of future, our fates align.

Lips match rhythm in an adoring trance,
Fueling the fire of a fairy-tale romance.
Drawn together by the gravity of heart,
In intoxicating interlace, we never part.

## Serenity's Sighing Sap

Beneath the bowers of solace we lie,
Where the willow's whispers softly ply.
The serenity's sap, it soothes our soul,
In nature's arms, we find ourselves whole.

Leaves murmur secrets in rustling tones,
A lullaby through which tranquility roams.
The brook babbles with a gentle clap,
Singing hymns of serenity's sap.

Our breaths mingle with the cooling breeze,
Carrying away our worries with ease.
In this moment, time's grip we can elapse,
As we recline in serenity's sap.

## Companion's Candied Concoction

Friendship's essence, sweetly fused,
In laughter’s echo, we’re amused.
A blend of moments, shared confection,
In companion's candied connection.

With every jest and fleeting glance,
We brew a history, rich by chance.
Sprinkled with sugar, tales untold,
In the syrup of stories, bond grows bold.

Cheers we chime in sparkling light,
To the sweetness that makes hearts ignite.
Joined by the candied threads we weave,
In shared concoction, we believe.

## Affection's Aromatic Blend

Whispers soft as petals fall,
Beneath the moon's tender gaze.
Gentle touches rise and stall,
In the night's serene embrace.

Love's aroma in the air,
Intertwining hearts in flight.
Silken tendrils of maiden hair,
Dance in love's enchanting light.

Eyes that sparkle, stars aligned,
Sighs that mingle with the breeze.
Two souls gracefully entwined,
Sharing whispered pleasantries.

Harmony in passion's play,
Senses yield to sweet command.
In this blend, love finds its way,
By the warmth of affection's hand.

## Embrace's Enchanted Distill

In the still of our embrace,
Time surrenders to our touch.
Every worry we erase,
In this moment's gentle clutch.

Words unspoken, feelings spun,
Hearts converse without a sound.
In the space where two are one,
Peace and solace can be found.

Wrapped in solitude's own keep,
Spirits soar on love's soft wing.
Bound by bonds both rich and deep,
To each other's souls we cling.

Casting spells no eye can see,
Magical as night's first chill.
Nothing matches, nor can be,
Like embrace's enchanted distill.

## Romance's Rare Concoction

Elixirs of ancient lore,
Cannot match the love we pour.
The tender look that we exchange,
Ignites a fire, deep and strange.

Fingers laced with silent prayer,
For a love beyond compare.
Moonlight bathes us in its glow,
Romance blossoms, sweet and slow.

Lips that whisper sweetened verse,
Bind our hearts, for better or worse.
In this cup, we both partake,
Savoring the love we make.

Alchemy of purest form,
Romance against the norm.
Rare concoction, potent spell,
In our love, we're lost and well.

## Connection's Chemistry Cure

Atoms dancing in the night,
Forming bonds both loose and tight.
Mystery in love's allure,
Chemistry becomes the cure.

Emotions blend, reaction starts,
Drawing near two beating hearts.
In the vessel of our trust,
Connection turns the iron to rust.

Elements of you and me,
Combine to form a unity.
Prescriptions of the past we shed,
On newfound paths our souls are led.

Potions fail to imitate,
The love that we originate.
With every hug, each loving stare,
Connection's chemistry we share.

## Consort's Cordial Cure

In quiet cloisters of the heart's expanse,
A consort's gentle touch begins the dance.
The cordial cure for solitude's sharp lance,
Where paired pulses beat in tender trance.

With whispers shared in night's soft, sibilant hiss,
Two souls converge in a cocoon of bliss.
The balm of presence, none other can dismiss,
A remedy sealed with a honeyed kiss.

No ailment of the spirit could endure,
When shared with one whose intentions are pure.
In love's own chalice, the sweetest liqueur,
A consort's cordial cures, for sure.

## Yearning's Yeasty Yield

In the oven of aspirations high,
Desire's dough, under the warmth, shall rise.
Puffed up with dreams beneath the azure sky,
The scent of hope in the gusty breeze lies.

Yearning's yeast works its vigorous spell,
Turning the mundane to creations rare.
With every swell, a story it will tell,
A chronicle of love and fervent care.

Harvest the grain of passion's fervent field,
Knead it with vigor; to fate, do not yield.
Bake in the hearth of perseverance sealed,
Yearning's yeasty bounty is revealed.

## Accord's Ambrosial Ale

From the cauldron of disparate souls,
A potion's brewed, harmony's foremost goal.
In the tavern of unity, bellied bowls,
Pour forth Accord's ambrosial ale, whole.

Each draught, a gulp of understanding's grace,
Disagreements dissolve in its embrace.
Hearts synchronize in time's measured pace,
Toasting to peace in life's interlace.

Raise your stein to the sky, savor each sip,
Let the ale of accord sweetly slip.
On the tongue of society, let it drip,
For in unity, we're kin in fellowship.

## Kinship's Kettle Karo

A family's fabric, finely interwoven,
Each thread supports the tapestry complete.
In kinship's kettle, love unspoken,
A slow simmering of connections sweet.

Generations stir the pot with care,
Adding spices of experience and age.
Whispers of ancestors flavor the air,
With every spoonful, heritage engage.

The karo thickens, rich and robust,
A testament to bonds that time has trust.
Within the hearth, amidst the ember's dust,
Kinship's kettle sings, in warmth we're just.

## Heart's Distillation

In chambers deep where whispers dwell,
Like echoes in a crystal shell,
Essence pure, emotions swell,
A distillation, love's sweet spell.

A serenade of heartbeat's chime,
In rhythm with a soul's rhyme,
Each throb a drop of time,
Sieved through memory's prime.

The alchemy of joy and pain,
Mixtures rich with love's deep strain,
Each tear and smile, a gain,
In distillation, nothing's in vain.

This heart of mine, a vat so true,
Refining feelings, old and new,
Transmuting moments through and through,
A spirit's brew, in shades of hue.

## Silent Adoration

In silence loud as roaring sea,
A heart's adoration, soft and free,
No words spoken, yet hearts agree,
An unvoiced bond, like a sacred decree.

In gaze that lingers, souls converse,
Silent love, a universe,
Unheard symphony, tender and terse,
A vow profound, beyond rehearse.

Eyes whisper what lips dare not say,
In silent adoration, hearts sway,
A quiet promise held at bay,
In mute allegiance, love's display.

With every breath, the silent sound,
Of love’s vibration, profound,
In silence, our spirits are bound,
In adoration, without a word found.

## Serenade of Senses

A touch ignites, a fiery bloom,
Hands speak, in silent room,
Love's serenade, does consume,
Senses dancing, to an ancient tune.

A scent that lingers in the air,
Like whispers of a floral prayer,
A serenade so faint, so fair,
Enchants the night with fragrant flair.

Taste of nectar, sweet on lips,
As in a fervent, loving eclipse,
The serenade of senses slips,
Into a dance of soulful scripts.

Sound of breaths, in harmony,
A symphony for you and me,
Serenade of senses, a melody,
In chords of shared intimacy.

## Kiss of Essence

A kiss so light, upon the breeze,
Nature’s breath, an essence to seize.
A touch from petals, with such ease,
A moment's capture, hearts to please.

Softly treading through the mist,
Where droplets and dawn have kissed,
An essence pure, cannot be missed,
A moment in time, sweetly tryst.

Sensations tender as morning dew,
The essence of life, as if on cue,
A kiss from the universe, broad and true,
Invigorating souls, through and through.

This kiss of essence, a sacred rite,
A blend of shadows in the light,
An eternal bond, holding tight,
In the symphony of day and night.

## Brewed in Bond

In vats of trust, our friendship brews,
Where time and patience blend the hues.
Aged with laughter, a hearty cheer,
Each sip we take, our bond renews.

Shared secrets in the dead of night,
Whispers 'neath the pale moonlight.
Confidences poured out and sworn,
In the solace of our foresight.

Through trials, our spirits did clash,
Yet settled like the gentlest ash.
In unity, our hearts combine,
The strongest bond, no force can dash.

As barrels hold the finest drink,
Our friendship, too, shall never shrink.
Brewed in bond, a lifetime's worth,
A testament in every clink.

## Desire's Draft

Desire's draft, a subtle quill,
Traces need where will is still.
In pensive strokes the heart does spill,
Upon the page, it seeks its thrill.

The ink, it flows like passions tide,
With every line, our dreams confide.
A rendezvous the words provide,
A whispering place where hearts abide.

The scent of yearning on each page,
A story of the souls wage.
Beneath the lines, emotions cage,
Desire's draft, the ageless sage.

This potion scribed, love's pure motif,
In hidden words and silent belief.
Brimming cups of joy and grief,
In every drop, lies sweet relief.

## Muted Yearnings

Silent whispers in the crowd,
Muted yearnings speak aloud.
Hopes enshrouded in a shroud,
Dreams in dusky clouds are bowed.

Eyes that converse, words unspoken,
Promises made, yet none are broken.
Gentle glances, love's soft token,
In silence, vast desires woken.

Beating hearts with muffled cries,
Longing in the quiet lies.
Underneath the stoic skies,
Veiled wishes in disguise.

Yet in the hush, a truth discerns,
As the silent heart still yearns.
In the quietude it turns,
For the touch for which it burns.

## Love's Concoction

A dash of smiles, a pinch of tears,
Blended hopes with intertwined fears.
A stirring of the passing years,
In love's concoction, sweet and fierce.

Whispers soft as morning's dawn,
Feelings deep as oceans yawn.
In the crucible we're drawn,
Alchemy from dusk till morn.

With every heartbeat's tender thread,
Through every word unsaid.
In every blush of rosy red,
Our hearts and souls are gently led.

Time's elixir, potent brew,
In the chalice, me and you.
Sipping on the morning dew,
Our love, eternal, ever new.

**Whispers of Affection**

In the silence of the night, my dear,
Soft echoes of our love appear.
Gentle words that touch the heart,
Binding souls that never part.

Underneath the moon's soft glow,
Love's sweet whispers softly flow.
Across the darkness, to your ear,
They travel close, from far to near.

Through every whisper, feelings twine,
In every line, your name with mine.
A quiet symphony so sweet,
Where whispers of affection meet.

Each murmur is a tender kiss,
A moment filled with purest bliss.
Our whispered love, forever strong,
In each soft word, where we belong.

## Midnight's Potion

A brew of stars in skies so black,
Concoction deep where light lacks.
Stir the cauldron of the night,
Midnight's potion, dark delight.

Moonlight's silver stirs the blend,
With velvet darkness as its friend.
A sip of cosmos, infinite span,
Drunk by the eyes of every man.

Galactic mist and comet's tail,
In this potion, dreams set sail.
A celestial elixir pure,
In midnight's hands, the heart secures.

This heady draft in heavens cast,
A spell of night that ever lasts.
Enchanting souls until the dawn,
When Midnight's Potion lingers on.

## Tender Brews

In the morning's quiet hours,
Awake a blend of fragrant flowers.
A tender brew of petals sweet,
Where colors, scents, and daylight meet.

Stirring slow the morning breaks,
While dew adorns the earth it makes.
Each droplet, nature's gentle brew,
Reflects the dawn in crystal hue.

A flourishing of life anew,
The tender brew of morning dew.
With gentle hand the sun will touch,
And warm the earth it loves so much.

The world awakes, a day to prove,
Of tender moments, soft and smooth.
This earthly tea poured out for you,
The daily brew of life, anew.

## Embrace Infusion

In the warmth of close embrace,
We find a sweet and tranquil place.
A fusion of two hearts in thrall,
Each other's harbor, standing tall.

The mix of laughs, of tears, of dreams,
Creates a bond that ever gleams.
In this infusion, love's own space,
Is built within our hearts' own grace.

Emotions blend, a potent tea,
Each sip a part of you and me.
Strength and comfort in this blend,
An infusion that will never end.

Holding tight in love's collusion,
We share our lives, our sweet infusion.
In every touch, in every gaze,
We celebrate our endless days.

## Sentimental Spirits

In the hush of twilight's gentle sigh,
Where shadows dance and spirits fly.
A tender touch on memories old,
Silent stories that hearts hold.

Beneath the moon's soft silver hue,
Longings stir within the dew.
Whispers of the past that cling,
To sentimental spirits that sing.

The night air carries a loving trace,
Of vanished smiles, an embrace.
In dreams these quiet specters weave,
A tale of love that never leaves.

Each wistful ghost in starlight draped,
Recounts the joys that once escaped.
In the silence, their fond pleas,
Drift like leaves on autumn’s breeze.

## Potion of Proximity

A brew of closeness, mixed so sweet,
With every heartbeat, skips a beat.
An elixir, clear as the sky,
Draws us closer, you and I.

In each drop, a moment's flare,
The space between us thins to air.
Potion of proximity imbibe,
To our whispered dreams subscribe.

Sipped with eyes locked, full and deep,
The distance fades, we're no longer steep.
With every swallow, nearer we glide,
On the voyage where our souls confide.

Intertwined in silent lore,
The potion works its magic sure.
No longer two but merged as one,
Proximity's potion, its work now done.

## Warmth in a Whisper

A whisper in the cold, a delicate refrain,
It carries the warmth, a gentle balm for pain.
Words soft-spoken, in the night's ear,
A soothing melody for hearts to hear.

Each syllable a spark, igniting the air,
A dance of embers, bright and fair.
The chill recedes with every word,
As if within, a sun's been stirred.

The voice of a loved one, a tender hiss,
Can thaw a frost with a single kiss.
In that breath, a summer's day,
Where love's warm whispers come to play.

The cold world may bring its harshest whisper,
But warmth endures in soft-spoken timber.
In every quiet word, love's power sings,
Adrift on air, on golden wings.

## Enamored Alchemy

With whispered words, the spell begins,
Mixing emotions, feeling spins.
An alchemist of heart's desire,
Turns the mundane into fire.

Love's ingredients in a blend,
Each gesture, glance, a message send.
Poured into the crucible's glow,
From common lead to gold, it flows.

Transmutation of a single touch,
Cherished moments mean so much.
Alchemy of the enamored kind,
Seeking the treasure that hearts find.

In the lab of intertwined hands,
Chemistry becomes more than plans.
Enamored alchemy's sweet thrill,
Crafted with passion, love’s skill.

## Caress's Cup

In tender touches, warmth imbibes,
A subtle shiver, skin describes,
Gentle as dawn's first light that gilds,
The caress's cup, with love it builds.

Feathered strokes paint silent speech,
In every curve they softly reach,
A liquid language, free and deep,
In this cup, our promises keep.

The rim, where lips do meet and part,
A sip of union from the heart,
Fingers laced as threads of fate,
In this cup, our touch creates.

Held within two palms' embrace,
A vessel of our love's own grace,
Elixer from the purest source,
Within this cup, love charts its course.

## Fervor's Flask

Contained within this fervor's flask,
A potion bold, no questions asked,
It bubbles with a fiery zest,
A brew of passion, unexpressed.

Each swallow filled with yearning's flame,
Igniting hearts to call one name,
A draught so potent, fearless, wild,
Within this flask, desire's child.

It warms the veins with urgent need,
For every whispered pledge to heed,
It dances on the drinker's tongue,
Fervor's Flask, forever young.

With every sip, a pledge is made,
To chase the night, to never fade,
A toast to ardor, strong and true,
In this flask, love's fervor brew.

## Whispers of the Heart's Potion

In silence steeped, this hushed elixir,
Whispers of the heart, tender and richer,
Sipped in solitude, or shared with another,
In this potion's path, feelings uncover.

A gentle murmur, a quiet night,
In the potion's depths, stars alight,
A symphony soft, of the soul's wishing,
Soothing as the moon, love's hushing fishing.

The secret notes this potion plays,
Of inner desires, and innermost frays,
It calms the turmoil, brightens the notion,
From this heartfelt draft, the deepest emotion.

Drink to the silence, to the soft-spoken word,
To the thoughts unvoiced, yet inwardly heard,
In each drop a whisper, of love's pure devotion,
This is the essence, the heart's own potion.

## Love's Secret Brew

Beneath the surface, passions churn,
A secret potion, for which we yearn,
In hidden depths, it simmers true,
An alchemy of me and you.

Its recipe a mystery,
Of glances, smiles, a touch, a plea,
A concoction made of sweet rapport,
Love's Secret Brew, who could want more?

Aged in trust's oaken cask,
A delicate, yet sturdy flask,
With each taste, a revelation,
A quiet storm of adoration.

A sip for courage, a draught for cheer,
In love's own brew, we find our seer,
A tonic for the heart's own quest,
In this brew, love's secrets rest.

## Tenderness's Tasty Transfusion

Soft whispers stroke the embered sky,
Like silk against the evening's sigh.
Caring touches, a gentle hush
A moment's peace, the world's soft brush.

Tenderness spills in the night,
A banquet for the soul's delight.
Each gesture, a flavor so sweet,
In every heartbeat, lovers meet.

The world's cacophony grows dim,
As kindness fills to the brim.
In every look, and every fusion,
Is found the taste of love's transfusion.

Eyes meet and dance in silent song,
Where only hearts may truly belong.
A tender feast, so pure, so true,
In every shade of love's own hue.

## Sentience in Solvent

Drowned in thoughts, a solvent sea,
Conscious waves ebb endlessly.
Selves adrift, each mind a reef,
Sifting through belief and grief.

The mind's eye bleeds in conscious streams,
Tossing through our thoughts and dreams.
In the wash of wondering wave,
Is where our deepest selves we save.

To fathom sentient ocean's depth,
All truths and doubts herein are kept.
Awake within this liquid skin,
The self unfolds from where it's been.

Our essence swims in solvent's grace,
In every mind, a sacred space.
Eternal flow of pure cognition,
Each sentience, its own audition.

## Ethereal Embrace Elixir

In the quiet of the twilight mist,
Where stars and souls tenderly kiss.
Lies an essence, fine and rare,
The elixir of the air.

A draught of the ether's own embrace,
Carries the heart to a higher place.
With each sip, unseen threads entwine,
In a dance of the divine.

Gentle and soft, the potion soars,
Unlocking hidden celestial doors.
Within its hold, the spirit's lease,
On the pieces of eternal peace.

Drink deep of this celestial brew,
Let the sky's own heart filter through.
This elixir, with its whispering light,
In its hold, the soul takes flight.

## Pairing's Perfumed Potion

Aroma sweet, the scent of two,
Blended in a fragrant dew.
Like roses in a twin bouquet,
Together, in a scented ballet.

Two souls, their essence in a jar,
Like twining vines that never are far.
A potion steeped in shared lives' motion,
Bound by love's deep, perfumed ocean.

Silent whispers in the phial,
Each breath a chapter in the tale.
Suspended in the liquid dance,
In every drop, romance's chance.

Cheers to the potion, the paired infusion,
In its scent, no sight of seclusion.
The bottle of joy, tightly corked,
Where two fragrances are beautifully forked.

## Charm's Chalice

In the alcove of allure, the goblet gleams,
A vessel filled with liquid dreams.
Its curves are etched with tales of yore,
Whispering secrets of the lore.

Velvet red within the cup doth swirl,
A dance of fate, a misty twirl.
The drink, a blend of mirth and chance,
Invites the heart to an enchanted dance.

Who sips from this, the chalice deep,
Shall find the charm they're meant to keep.
For in the potion, lies the spell,
The magic's touch they'll know too well.

Drink deep and feel the charm arise,
The chalice's gift, a cherished prize.
In just one draught, you may perceive,
The wonders that you can achieve.

## Soulmate's Syrup

Upon the lips, the syrup sweet,
Two souls in silent serendipity meet.
A flavor shared in the space between,
A taste of love, pure and serene.

Its essence captures a bond so rare,
In the syrup's sheen, they find a pair.
Through every drop, the spirit sings,
Connecting hearts with gossamer wings.

Each sip is laced with love's own muse,
Soothing the hearts, it gently infuses.
The glow it kindles never slips,
For soulmate's love is eternal bliss.

Bound in the brew, the syrup tells,
Of a timeless dance where true love dwells.
Drink to the promise that love assures,
In soulmate's syrup, the bond endures.

## Blossoms of Bliss

In gardens of serenity, the flowers bloom,
A perfumed breath, a sweet perfume.
Petals unfurl in the gentle kiss,
Welcoming you to blossoms of bliss.

Each hue and shade, a vibrant verse,
Nature's beauty, the universe.
They dance in breeze, with tender sway,
In harmony, they spend their day.

The lilies sing with the roses blush,
In silent symphony, a tranquil hush.
With every bloom, the heart is given,
A glimpse of paradise, a piece of heaven.

So, wander through these verdant aisles,
Where bliss bespeaks in floral styles.
With each blossom's gentle hiss,
Find solace in their blissful kiss.

## Quiet Quench

In the whisper of the evening's breath,
Through quietude where shadows wreathe.
The soul finds a stream so lea,
In placid sips, it seeks to be free.

Quench, oh quench, the thirsting mind,
In gentle torrents, peace we find.
The silence is our sweetest draught,
In its embrace, our cares are laught.

The hush descends, a loving shroud,
In the quiet quench, the heart is vowed.
To sip from stillness, oh so rich,
Where whispers weave without a hitch.

So drink from the silence, deeply now,
Let the quietude be your sacred vow.
The tranquility, a thirst that quells,
In every drop, the silence tells.

## Adoration's Ambient Elixir

In the heart where love’s light lingers,
Softly in its tender keep,
Every sigh and touch that fingers,
Lends the soul its restful sleep.

Through the night, the stars do whisper,
Silent songs of sweet affection,
Moonlit dance on skin does shimmer,
Adoration's pure reflection.

Gentle draft from lips anointing,
Sipping slow the ambient draft,
Calm the chest once tight, now pointing,
To the sky once wept, now laughed.

Inhale deep of love's own essence,
Feel its warmth without the pyre,
Boundless comfort, soft and presence,
Heart embraced by passion’s fire.

**Fondness's Fermented Fantasy**

In vats of dreams our fondness lies,
Fermenting 'neath a watchful guise,
A bouquet rich, notes bold and free,
Aged to perfection, like memory.

Fleeting glances, tender traces,
In aging casks find their spaces,
Time enriches what we feel,
Fantasy becomes the real.

Sip the nectar of desire,
Vintage visions, ever higher,
Bottled bliss in longing's dance,
Grapes of whimsy given chance.

Laced with laughter, steeped in thought,
Each sip a chapter, love has wrought,
Uncork the spirit, let it flow,
Fondness’s vintage, hearts aglow.

## Whispered Wishes in a Bottle

Upon the glass, soft breath condenses,
Whispered wishes, heart's defenses,
Lowered slowly, one by one,
In a bottle, set to sun.

Tossed to waves of fate's own making,
Messages of hope, awaking,
Drifting far on seas unknown,
To find a shore where love has flown.

Echoes of a soul's deep yearning,
In the vessel, softly turning,
Words like sailors, brave and true,
Seeking ports of view anew.

Bespoke dreams in liquid letters,
Borne upon the briny betters,
Someday to be found again,
And answered by a kindred pen.

## Cupid's Crafted Cure-All

With cherub's bow and arrow deft,
He mixes mirth and weaves the weft,
Cupid’s cure-all, craft so pure,
Heals the hearts that plead demure.

In the cauldron of his making,
Passion’s potion gently shaking,
Stirs in joy with blush of cheek,
Given to the love they seek.

Sip of this and no more ail,
Amour’s remedy to prevail,
Kissed with sweetness, touched with flair,
Cupid’s blend, none else compare.

Love now courses through each vein,
Elixir of the heart's own reign,
Cupid toasts his crafted art,
With draught that mends the fractured heart.

## Close Quarters Cocktail

In this glass, a blend confined,
So close, the flavors intertwined,
A sip of closeness, zests combined,
Intimate concoction, perfectly designed.

Four walls embrace our festive cheer,
Intimacy blooms when you are near,
With each clink, a toast sincere,
Close quarters cocktail, our sphere.

Citrus tang and spirits dance,
A fusion bold, left not to chance,
In the clasp of a crowded stance,
We savor the serendipitous romance.

Jubilant laughter fills our nook,
Our shared tales in each look,
In the cradle of our snug rook,
The world outside, we gently forsook.

## Sentiment's Scented Solution

Fragrant droplets, memories steep,
In the heart's crypts, they softly seep,
Aromatic whispers, do awaken sleep,
In sentiment's scented solution, we leap.

Blossoms bottled in liquid form,
A scent evokes, a past reborn,
Each note plays an emotive horn,
In this perfumed mist, our senses adorn.

Vapors of vanilla, musk's embrace,
Odors paint a long-lost place,
Scented ghosts, we gently chase,
In each inhalation, time's trace.

Through olfactory gates, emotions pour,
Diffusing through every pore,
In scents we find, the moments yore,
With every breath, we explore.

## Warmth's Whispered Potion

A draught of heat in winter's grip,
From the cauldron, a steamy sip,
Weave the warmth of fellowship,
In the mug of kinship we dip.

Hear the embers' hushed confessions,
Crackling with life's impressions,
Flames that fuel our night's sessions,
Their glow, our tranquil obsession.

With a blanket's tender embrace,
We face the hearth, heart's fireplace,
Each spark adds to our inner grace,
In the warmth, our troubles erase.

Cozy whispers twirl and mix,
As logs transform to candlesticks,
The potion soothes with gentle licks,
Our spirits raised with fiery tricks.

## Bonds of Botanical Bliss

In the garden where affections bloom,
Petals reflect the moon's costume,
Threads of flora in nature's loom,
We're entwined in the botanical room.

Roots of friendship delve so deep,
In this grove of souls we keep,
Symbiotic lives, tangled heap,
In verdant bonds, forever steep.

Leaves that whisper in the breeze,
Share the secrets of the trees,
Our unity, the birds and bees,
In botanical bliss, we find our ease.

Nature's grasp, firm yet tender,
Grows a bond that none can render,
Amidst the blooms, we surrender,
To the earth, our ephemeral sender.

## Unity's Unspoken Draft

Whispering winds weave the silent thread,
Unity’s dance in every spread,
Harmonious hearts, the distance defied,
Unseen arms of fate allied.

In unity's unspoken draft, we soar,
Leaving behind the solitary shore,
Together we rise, together we draft,
A mosaic of souls, masterfully crafted.

Beneath the same sky, we dream as one,
A tapestry of life, brilliantly spun,
Each thread unique, yet jointly cast,
In the unspoken draft, unity's hold fast.

No words are needed for this invisible lace,
It wraps the world in its silent embrace,
Hearts entwined in a tender ballet,
In unity's draft, we find our way.

## Silent Symphony of Senses

A hush descends, the senses peak,
An orchestra of silence speaks,
Aroma's whisper, texture's tune,
A silent symphony beneath the moon.

Eyes closed, the world's unheard ballet,
A canvas painted in shades of grey,
Touch and taste, the leaders' hum,
In this silent symphony, we become one.

The rustle of leaves, a silent note,
A shiver of light, softly smote,
Whispering grasses in gentle sway,
Compose the quiet display.

Unplayed keys within the heart,
Where silent songs do impart,
Inaudible crescendos rise and fall,
The senses' symphony, enthralls us all.

## Touch's Transcendent Tea

Fingertips brush like whispers of lace,
A porcelain cup, a tender embrace,
Warmth that seeps to the spirit deep,
In touch's transcendent tea, we steep.

Gentle hands pour out solace's brew,
A mingling of souls in this silent hue,
A sip of connection, no words can claim,
In touch's warmth, we're never the same.

Skin to skin, the world fades away,
In the quiet steep, where fingers play,
A tea of comfort, no barriers keep,
Touch's brew runs marvelously deep.

So hold me close, let the infusion flow,
Where touch transcends and feelings grow,
The cup of companionship never too steep,
In touch's transcendent tea, bonds leap.

## Infatuation's Flavorful Fount

A gaze that lingers, sweet and profound,
An elixir from infatuation’s flavorful fount,
Each glance, each smile, stirs the brew,
A concoction of longing, ever so true.

With every heartbeat, the flavor grows,
In a blush’s bloom, affection shows,
Tastebuds tingle with each thought,
In infatuation’s fount, we're caught.

Lips part, taking in the taste,
A mingling of hearts, not a single waste,
Savoring the moments in passion’s clout,
Drunk on the fount, love’s sprout.

So sip on the sweet nectar of desire,
Let infatuation’s fount set hearts afire,
Imbibe the essence, pure and devout,
In the flavorful fount, love’s route.

## Bedazzled by Beverages

In crystal glasses, liquors twirl,
Amidst the chatter of the night.
Each sip whispers secrets swirled,
Under the bar’s soft, mellow light.

Amber ale with frothy grace,
Gleams like gems in dim-lit spaces.
Ruby wine with silent cheer,
Brings the warmth of distant places.

Spirits dance in liquid haze,
Jazz and laughter interlace.
Silver streams of bubbles rise,
Moments in their effervesce.

Mix and blend the flavors bold,
Tales of bitterness untold.
Sweet or sour on the tongue,
Bedazzled, every drink is gold.

## Murmuring Myrrh of Mirth

Whispers softly in the air,
The scent of myrrh is laughing fair.
Aromas swirl, and in their wake,
Merry tales begin to bake.

A hint of humor in each breath,
It curls and lingers after death.
Into the soul it gently seeps,
And from the heart, it warmly leaps.

It dances on the evening’s tongue,
Serenades by old songs sung.
Every whiff a fragrant mirth,
An ancient pleasure given birth.

So breathe in deep the resin's song,
Its murmured joy can do no wrong.
Let it fill you, spurn all strife,
With murmuring myrrh, enrapture life.

## Sentimental Sip of Sunrise

The crimson dawn spills in my cup,
With streaks of gold to stir it up.
Each gulp, a blend of early light,
A sip of sun to break the night.

The zephyr's cool, the earth is still,
With misty dreams the air does fill.
Sweet dew upon the grass does weep,
As morning sighs from slumber’s deep.

A sip for hope, a gulp for grace,
The sun ascends at steady pace.
With every draught, the sky’s new blush,
Gives life’s routine a gentle flush.

So here’s to skies that turn so bright,
A toast to day dispelling night.
A sentimental sip of dawn,
In quietude, a new day born.

## Revelry's Refined Remedy

Raise a glass to nights that gleam,
With laughter, joy, and silver stream.
A taste of revelry so kind,
In sips of refined remedy find.

Let merriment be the potion sweet,
That steadies heart and guides the feet.
Dance away the aches and woes,
In the elixir that freely flows.

Forget the toil, forget the pain,
In the alchemy of champagne.
Each bubble bursts with tale and jest,
A fleeting remedy at best.

So drink to peace, to love, to cheer,
With friends and kin always near.
In revelry's kind, tender balm,
Find solace, comfort, and calm.

## Romance's Remedy

In twilight's amber glow, hearts entwine,
Whispers soft as silk, in night's embrace.
Candlelight flickers, shadows fine,
In love's tender gaze, solace we trace.

Eyes meet, unspoken hopes to confess,
Gentle touches, the language of care.
Two souls blend in seamless caress,
Finding in each, a solace rare.

Beneath the moon's silver crescent beam,
Promises forged in the hush of eve.
In every sigh, a reverent dream,
Romance's remedy we weave.

Wistful nights, where heartaches once dwelled,
Healing whispers, love's lore compelling.
In the sanctuary of arms upheld,
Peace blooms where once there was a quelling.

## Velvet Drafts

In the quietude of the dimming light,
Velvet drafts sweep through the open sash.
Words unspoken fill the air of night,
In every stroke, a painter's dash.

Leaves rustle with soft, secret tones,
Dancing to the rhythm of the breeze.
While in the shadows, nature hones,
A symphony among the trees.

Gentle gusts, the sentinels of dusk,
Carry tales from lands far and near.
In the embrace of the evening's musk,
Every breath we take is clear.

In the silence, the velvet drafts speak,
Scripts of air, bold and yet so meek.
Echoes of the forest, strong and sleek,
Writing stories for the hearts that seek.

## Passion's Philter

In the cauldron of desire, a brew so rare,
Mixing essences of fire, with tender care.
Sipped from the chalice of lovers' lips,
In the potion, the heart eagerly dips.

Flames dance in the eyes of the enthralled,
Each glance, a spell that cannot be stalled.
Passion's philter, a powerful potion,
Stirring the soul with unbridled emotion.

Through veins it flows, a liquid flame,
Igniting whispers of a love untamed.
From this draught, entwined fates conspire,
Kindling the blaze of fervent fire.

In the silence, fervor spoken loud,
In every touch, the passion endowed.
With every sip from the lover's vial,
Eternal flames are set to spiral.

## Secret Amour

In the garden of whispers, our secret blooms,
Amidst the roses veiled in nocturnal perfumes.
Tender is the night that shrouds our encounter,
Underneath the stars that gaze and ponder.

Shadows caress our silent reverie,
As we dance to love's ancient melody.
The world unaware of the hearts we've poured,
In every embrace, our amour is stored.

Whispered terms of endearment, softly spoken,
Within our haven, no vows are broken.
Secret amour, the clandestine flame,
In the quiet, we call each other's name.

Yet when the dawn with her fingers rosy,
Calls forth the day, so bright and nosy,
Safely tucked away our passion lies,
In the hush-hush of our sunset sighs.

## Touch's Tranquility

In whispers of the weeping willow's sway,
A tender touch, calm's orchestra does play.
In gentle grasp, a peace so soft and still,
Serenity's caress, the world's own quill.

Fingertips like brushes dip in dreams,
Sketching comfort's canvas, quiet streams.
Silent symphony of skin on skin,
Harmony in hold, where trust begins.

Beneath the chaos, constant, rushing roar,
Your touch, the tranquil shore that I adore.
In your embrace, my worries unfurl, fly,
In the silent sanctuary we lie.

The warmth exchanged, not fire but glowing embers,
A silent language, every soul remembers.
Touch's tranquil tale, in tender tones it tells,
In every outlined arch, serenity dwells.

## Sighs of Sweetness

Oh, the sighs of sweetness fill the air,
Rising like the incense's whispered prayer.
Each breath a verse of love's enchanting song,
Where hearts confess that they've belonged all along.

The breezes hum the chorus through the trees,
Carrying our sighs with effortless ease.
Passions penned in every whispered gale,
Stories shared where words would often fail.

The night sky listens to our silent voice,
As stars twinkle, echoing our rejoice.
In every sigh, a sweetness so profound,
Love's language in its purest form is found.

Sweetness in each sigh, a secret kiss,
A silent melody of blissful bliss.
In echo's gentle cadence, love's own art,
Enshrined within the beating of our heart.

## Nectar of Nearness

In the garden of closeness, blooms delight,
Where the nectar of nearness tastes just right.
The buzzing bees of longing come to feast,
On the proximity, love increased.

Every petal soft, against my skin,
Pollen's dust of touch, letting you in.
Sap sweet on the tongue, a taste treasured,
In each moment, our closeness is measured.

Vines of intimacy twine with grace,
In the nectar of nearness, we embrace.
Through the orchards of our whispered chats,
Grow the fruits of fondness where love now sits.

Near enough to hear each quiet breath,
Where the essence of affection is kept.
In the nearness, a nectar so pure,
A bond's sweetness, forever to endure.

## Brew for Two

Steam spirals softly from cups intertwined,
In the brew for two, our lives are combined.
A sip of shared warmth, in morning's first light,
Our love steeped deeply, chasing the night.

Curling steam writes tales in wisps above,
Whispers of flavors, steeped in our love.
With each shared cup, the blend grows richer,
Two souls in conversation's pitcher.

A blend of two hearts in one single mug,
Stronger together, a perfect hug.
The aroma of joy fills the room,
In our tiny haven, love's in bloom.

Daily ritual, simple and small,
Yet within it lies our story's thrall.
Brew for two, in perfect harmony,
In every drop, our love's symphony.

## Companionship's Concentrated Cordial

In fellowship's elixir, we find our hearts pour,
A meld of mirth in unity, it's you I adore.
Together steeped in trust, through life's demand,
Our spirits share the glass, from hand to hand.

Through laughs and tears, a blend so rich,
Each moment with you, my soul's bewitch.
In this drink, no solitude, no single life,
Companionship's cordial, through joy and strife.

Whispers of warmth in the cool night air,
We sip shared dreams, a double-seated chair.
Two lives entwined like vines that climb,
In the cordial of time, our friendship's rhyme.

A bond so deep, in kindred zest,
In this concentrated coziness, we are blessed.
Cheers, my friend, to the days we've spun,
In the cordial of us, our hearts are one.

## Twilight Tingle Tincture

Dusk's gentle potion, a tender gaze,
Of purple skies and amber blaze.
The eve's first star, a flicker faint,
An invitation the cosmos paint.

The Twilight tingle in ethereal light,
Beneath the crescent's chilling bite.
Cool whispers dance with night's approach,
In evening’s potion, stars encroach.

A tingle of peace, as shadows grow long,
The nightingale’s first twilight song.
As darkness settles, and critters stir,
Beneath the moon's silver fur.

The sky’s tincture, a tranquil brew,
A draught of cool in the fading blue.
Each sip of starlight, calm and bright,
Serenades the soul to the arms of night.

## Aurora's Amatory Absinth

With tender blush of first light's kiss,
Aurora whispers dawn's sweet bliss.
The skies alight with passion's hue,
An amorous blend of pink and blue.

The love of day and night's embrace,
In rosy glow, and nighttime's grace.
A torrid affair at dawn's own door,
A spectacle that one can't ignore.

Absinth of morning, a heady love,
Boundless skies that stretch above.
The larks sing high of romance's birth,
As light caresses the sleepy earth.

An infatuation with each new day,
In the breath of dawn, we quietly sway.
Aurora's passion in soft display,
Within this absinth, our hearts will stay.

## Felicity's Ferment

In the bubbling joy of Felicity's brew,
Each bubble a laugh, skipping anew.
In every sip, a spirited dance,
Moments savored, given the chance.

The zestful yeast of happiness ferments,
In the vats of life, no time for laments.
A toast to the things that make us gleam,
In Felicity’s concoction, we joyously dream.

With a hoppy heart, the malty mirth flows,
A golden ale of merriment grows.
Through the foamy head of carefree cheer,
Life’s beer's to drink without fear.

So raise your glass to the sky so clear,
In the ferment of happiness, we hold dear.
Let's drink to moments, so fleet and fast,
In the ale of joy, may our spirits last.

## Sensual Spirits Stirred

In twilight's tender hour, so soft and dim,
A gentle whisper dance, a serenade,
Each touch a language, words cannot impart,
Our senses mingle, in the dusk's cascade.

Two hearts in rhythmic tales of old and new,
A ballet of desires, unspoken thrills,
In every breath, a world of passion flares,
Beneath the moon, a story love instills.

The scent of roses in the air does swell,
With every petal's texture, sense delight,
Celestial canvas paints our silhouette,
Sensual spirits stirred into the night.

Starlight and shadow play upon our skin,
A symphony of moans, the breeze does stir,
The texture of your hair, a silken stream,
The taste of fervor's wine, sweet connoisseur.

## Emotion's Extract Embrace

Upon the canvas of my soul, you paint,
Emotions raw, in colors deep and true,
Each stroke imbues my being with your hue,
In your arms, I find my spirit quaint.

The warmth of kindled hearts in tight embrace,
Surrounding us with comfort's gentle sheath,
We speak in breaths, our chests in rise and fall,
Our trust weaves through the air, a tender wreath.

The tear that trickles from a joy so pure,
Emotion's extract running down my face,
It carves a path, a river of our grace,
In intertwining hearts, we are secure.

A laughter shared, the echoes form a choir,
In chambers of our laughter, love does bask,
No masks adorn our faces, simply ask,
And find in each reply, our true desire.

## Devotion's Delicate Draught

In the chalice of your love, I sip,
Devotion's delicate draught, divine,
Each drop, a pledge of forever clasp,
In sacred bond, our spirits align.

The taste of loyalty upon my tongue,
Steadfast and bold, like an ancient oak,
Rooted deep in soils of trust and care,
With every sip, in faith, we soak.

A promise in each small and subtle act,
A whisper of allegiance endures,
With every glance, a vow is renewed,
In love's own script, our epic assures.

Long years may pass, yet still the draught is sweet,
The cup refilled with each dawn's rosy light,
Through trials and smiles, our passion replete,
In devotion's cup, we find our might.

## Intimacy's Incantation

Whispered words, like spells, caress the air,
Intimacy's incantation, dear,
In the silence, secrets softly share,
Our bond, a mystic charm, does appear.

The gaze that holds a universe inside,
Transcending time, a bridge of souls is spun,
Eyes locked, a cosmic dance, no need to hide,
In sight's embrace, two beings become one.

A touch, a shudder, tracing lines of love,
A language only fingertips can speak,
Symbols etched upon the skin so soft,
In every gesture, intimacy peaks.

The quiet laughter, in the dead of night,
A symphony of joy in shared space,
Each note, a testament to our rite,
In closeness, we compose our own grace.

## Tender Tincture Serenade

Upon twilight's blush, does my heart parade,
With a tender tincture serenade.
In the hush of night, our whispers trade,
Entwined paths of starlight softly laid.

Beneath the moon's gentle, silver glow,
Echoes of affection begin to flow.
A symphony of silence in crescendo,
Casting love's aura with a tender glow.

Whispers of the nightingale, so sweet,
Singing tales where two fond hearts meet.
Surrendered to love's enchanting beat,
In this tender tincture, we find retreat.

The silent symphony carries our tune,
Under the watchful eye of the soothing moon.
Our serenade, a sacred, gentle boon,
Embodies the night in a tender swoon.

## Amour's Alchemical Essence

In vials of night, love's essence we distill,
A drop of dawn, a touch of twilight's thrill.
Chimeric potions, in our hearts instill,
The alchemy of amour, none can drill.

From whispered secrets, alchemist's skill,
Brewed in the cauldron, where dreams fulfill.
Fusions of feelings, a spectrum to spill,
Transmuting moments with a lover's will.

With every glance, a new compound forms,
Transforming spirits, as affection warms.
In the crucible of passion, magic storms,
Crafting elixirs that heartache deforms.

Our chemistry, no mere mortal understands,
In the alembic of embrace, love expands.
The essence of amour in intertwined hands,
A mystical merge, as destiny demands.

## Soul's Synergy Sips

Two souls in the chalice of night, they dip,
Intertwined fates take a synchronised sip.
In the goblet of stars, their essence equip,
A synergy's birth from a cosmic script.

Elixir of union, in timelessness grip,
Hearts converse in a celestial quip.
Mystical blend, as realities slip,
Sip by sip, into togetherness they flip.

Harmonious libation, a shared journey,
Tasting the vintage of a soul's tourney.
In each other's eyes, the world's sojourn, see,
A sip of you and me in eternity.

Celestial draughts of affinity we drain,
Quenching love's thirst, again and again.
Kinship imbibed, in heart's domain,
Soul's synergy, in every sip, we gain.

## Passion's Infused Drops

In the cauldron of dusk, with fervor we blend,
Passion's infused drops, in twilight's end.
Sparks of desire, with shadows they wend,
Mixing in whispers, as night skies ascend.

Droplets of ardor, time's fabric they rend,
Each touch, a fiery, lover's commend.
Two flames in a dance, they twist and bend,
In passion's concoction, our souls depend.

Every droplet, a universe of yearn,
Colliding cosmos, as stars burn.
Each drop, a lesson of love to learn,
In fervent fusion, for which we yearn.

A tapestry woven with passion's prose,
Infused with the essence that amour chose.
Through every touch, our desire grows,
In every drop, loves depth indisposed.

## Nostalgia's Nectarous Nip

Upon the memory's gentle tide we float,
Feeling the past’s warm whisper clothed in mist,
Old melodies play as from a distant boat,
In nostalgia's sweet, nectarous nip we're kissed.

Youth’s laughter echoes through the corridors of time,
Pebbled shores of moments, now distant and few,
Each tender tick resounds a nostalgic chime,
Rose-hued views tint our retrospectives anew.

Friends of old frolic in the mind's quiet glen,
Their shadows dance, twine in the soft glow of yore,
In the heart's silent movie, we watch again,
Reliving the embrace of days that are no more.

The air is rich with scents that once filled our breath,
Of places cherished, in the amber of the mind,
Nostalgia's kiss, sweet as the bloom of heath,
Through the nectarous nip, life's beauty we re-find.

## Solace's Soothing Spirits

In the hush of dusk, when the world softly sighs,
Solace whispers through the trees in tender tones,
Healing the hearts that the day's toil did agonize,
With soothing spirits, it gently soothes and atones.

Under the silver glow of a calming moon,
Solitude wraps its arms in a tranquil embrace,
Stars like confidants, to whom we quietly croon,
Amidst night's serenade, finds a peaceful place.

Echoes of the mind find quietude's reprieve,
Harboring in the haven where worries cease,
Through the spirits of solace, we believe,
In the quietude where restless thoughts find peace.

The soul's tumultuous seas grow still and calm,
While whispers of solace are like healing balm,
Breathing in repose, exhaling life's qualms,
In the realm of silence, a transcendent psalm.

## Attachment's Aperitif

Attachments stir the spirit, mix a poignant drink,
Ingredients of longing, garnished with a sigh,
In this aperitif, bittersweet we think,
Of the ties and bonds that we can't deny.

To the ones we cherish, from whom it's hard to part,
Like ivy, love clings and entwines the soul,
Each memory savored, an artful heart's tart,
Attachment’s libation, making us whole.

A sip of yearning, a draught of deep desire,
Toasting to the ones who our thoughts endear,
Connections brewing in a cauldron of fire,
Distilled through time, an attachment's clear cheer.

Drink deeply, for in these spirits we find,
The essence of presence, the expanse of care,
Aperitif to nourish the heart and mind,
In the throes of attachment, we're aware.

## Understanding's Unfolding Umber

In the shade of understanding, contemplation blooms,
Amidst the unfolding umber—a learning light,
Insight wends through the thoughts that it consumes,
Guiding through wisdom's hues, the path made bright.

Embrace the tapestry woven by knowing hands,
Threads of perception through the mind's loom glide,
With every strand, comprehension expands,
In the depth of umber, clarity resides.

Patience paints the canvas of cognizance,
With gentle strokes, revealing truths untold,
In shades of understanding, we find our stance,
And wisdom’s rich patina turns new to old.

Through the spectrum of though, we travel far,
In umber’s fold, we unfurl our sight,
Each lesson—a beacon, like a guiding star,
Illuminates our beings with understanding’s light.

## Memories in a Mix

In the quiver of leaves, the whisper winds,
Amidst the dance of stars, night's cloak pins.
Memory's tapestry, sewn with time's threads,
Melodies of old, where nostalgia treads.

Once upon a time seems not far to reach,
Each recollection a ripe, fleshy peach.
Fingers brush the velvet of the past,
Savoring moments too sweet to last.

Laughter echoes through corridors of thought,
Images unfurl, with sentiment fraught.
Jigsaw of the joyful, mosaic of the sad,
In the heart's museum, everything we've had.

Time's hands sift through our mental mix,
Choosing gems from a rubble of flicks.
Our lives but collages, past in frames,
In every heart, it's the memories that remains.

## Dedication's Dewy Distillate

Morning dew on the meadow's breast,
Efforts unseen, put to the test.
The toil of the dawn, painting petals anew,
Dedication's distillate, in the early light's hue.

Striving in silence, with secreted might,
Nurturing dreams in the faltering light.
Passion poured forth in pursuit of a quest,
In the sacrifice, life's true zest.

Steady hands craft the purpose of years,
In the forge of ambition, quenching fears.
The sweat becomes essence, fragrant and rife,
Enriching the soil of the garden of life.

The dew of resolve, on dawn's early leaf,
Heralds the harvest of honor's sheaf.
For persistence, in its hushed decree,
Is the dewy distillate of the devoted's decree.

## Lure of the Lingering Libation

In the chalice of chance, the liquid loops,
A siren's song, in spiraling swoops.
Intoxicating dance, of sips and sways,
The lure of the lingering libation plays.

Veiled in the vial, a potion to entice,
Vintage of vitality, spiced with vice.
A bubbling brew that beckons us taste,
The sweetness of life, not a drop to waste.

Raise the glass, where dreams dovetail,
Sailing on seas of a grape-flavored gale.
A sip of magic, under a moonlit sky,
Where whispers of love in the nightcap lie.

To toast to the memories, in amber waves,
In the warmth of the whisky, where longing craves.
The lure of the glass, forever may last,
The spirit's embrace holding hearts fast.

## Affinity's Aged Ambrosia

In the casks of kinship, time tends its treasure,
Maturing the moments of shared pleasure.
Affinity's ambrosia, in silence, it steeps,
In the bonds we brew, the spirit leaps.

Through years of aging, in darkened wood,
Flavors of fraternity, together stood.
In every sip, a history's told,
A reel of relations, in richness rolled.

The vintage of friendship, ripe and round,
In the depths of a bottle, camaraderie's found.
A toast to the souls that time has tied,
In the blend of brotherhood, trust is tried.

The bottle may empty, but not the affection,
Aged to perfection, beyond mere reflection.
Companionship's chalice, a brimming bounty,
Affinity aged, becomes our life's fountain.

## Ardor's Aperitif

In twilight's gentle grasping glow,
Our hearts entwine, set forth to show,
A sip of passion, love's first light,
Where shadows dance and fond hearts grow.

With every touch, the stars align,
Lips meet with Ardor's sweetest wine,
An aperitif of pure desire,
Two souls in twilight's soft confine.

Lights flicker in the banquet of night,
Promising love with every sight,
The prelude to a feast of hearts,
A toast to love, held ever tight.

In the silence, our whispers share,
Eager tastes of a love affair,
Ardor's Aperitif, we sip,
In the still of night, without a care.

## Solace Serum

When sorrow's grip is taut and cold,
And melancholy's tale is told,
A drop of Solace Serum sips,
Where warmth embraces, peace takes hold.

Upon the lips, it finds its way,
Ease the soul, keep the dark at bay,
A cure for hearts, in silent weep,
Where silent tears might cease to spray.

A potion of the tranquilest hue,
No more the sky of stormy blue,
Solace Serum soothes the mind,
And bathes life's canvas in calmer view.

In quietude, the spirit mends,
With each draught, the hurting ends,
Serum sweet, a liquid lullaby,
In its embrace, the broken bends.

## Embraceable Infusions

Gather 'round the cauldron's side,
Infusions rich where love won't hide,
Each stir, a spell, a tender thought,
In warm embrace, we all abide.

The potion bubbles, scents arise,
Heartfelt laughter, joyous cries,
Embraceable Infusions dance,
Underneath the moonlit skies.

A concoction brewed with care,
With every sip, it's love we share,
A liquid hug in every cup,
Unity found, a rare repair.

So drink it in, let worries cease,
In the broth of bonding, find your peace,
Infusions of embracing grace,
May the warmth of togetherness never cease.

## The Elixir of Us

In the chalice of our years,
The Elixir of Us appears,
Rich with laughter, steeped in tears,
A blend of love, overcoming fears.

Each sip, a memory's sweet caress,
An ode to joy, an admittance of stress,
The taste of all that we confess,
In the potion of our togetherness.

Through the seasons, our love proves tough,
Not always smooth, sometimes rough,
The elixir strong, undiluted, pure,
In its strength, our love endures.

So here's to us, a toast so just,
In every drop, in every gust,
Our shared life in this sacred cup,
The Elixir of Us, forever us.

## Soulmate's Sweet Serum

In whispers windswept and softly hummed,
A potion of love, in twilight's hour come.
Two hearts entwined in the moon's gentle gleam,
The soulmate's sweet serum, a shared dream.

Upon each sip, a tender touch unfurls,
In the dance of fate, as destiny swirls.
A sip of passion, where trust does redeem,
And whispers promise, of a mutual esteem.

In the vial of vigor, love's essence preserved,
Every drop, a sonnet, affection served.
Dreams are the currency that lovers deem,
Exchanged in glances, where silent words teem.

This concoction, a charm of the divine,
The elixir of us, where souls align.
In the chalice of unity, we glide upstream,
Savoring the sweetness of the infinite theme.

**Profound Pearls of Potables**

In the chalice of wisdom, spirits swirl,
Profound pearls of potables unfurl.
Each draught, a deep dive into the mind's well,
Where thoughts ferment and the heart can dwell.

A sip of insight, in liquid form found,
It carries one's senses to hallowed ground.
Whispers of history, in each vessel dwell,
Quaffing the chronicles that ancients tell.

The tapestry of tastes, a time-honored scroll,
In goblets of glass, they gently cajole.
Mastery in mixtures, a timeless spell,
Each potion, a story, waiting to compel.

So raise your glass to the enlightened soul,
Those profound pearls of potables console.
A tribute to truths that together gel,
In the communion of cups, where revelations swell.

## Velvet Vigor Vial

Within the velvet vigor vial's hold,
A tale of strength and bravery bold.
Sip by sip, it mends the weary heart,
Giving the spirit a vigorous start.

A concoction made of mettle and might,
A beacon that shines through the darkest night.
Its essence, a cure for the faltering part,
Restoring the zest that had once depart.

With each drop, the glass unveils its treasure,
A generous measure, beyond measure.
To the lips, a covenant to impart,
The art of vitality, ready to chart.

In the velvet vigor vial, behold the key,
Rousing the tired, setting their essence free.
Embarking anew, with courage at heart,
The elixir's promise forever to etch its part.

## Harmony's Honeyed Hydromel

From the hive of harmony, a nectar flows,
A hydromel so sweet, in golden glows.
Soothes the soul and sets the mind at ease,
Each sip a symphony, crafted to please.

Harmony's honeyed touch upon the tongue,
A melody savored, by old and young.
Through time it travels, a dulcet breeze,
Uniting all in peaceful reveries.

This honeyed hydromel, in goblets raised,
To the symphony of life, we have praised.
In unity, lips partake with gentle teas,
A chorus of hearts, in fluid harmonies.

Let the liquid gold fill our cups anew,
Savor harmony's hymn in this sacred brew.
With each sip, let us reconcile with ease,
In the honeyed harmony, our soul's crease.

## Trust's Treasured Tonic

A draught of sincerity poured from the soul,
A concoction so pure, it plays a vital role.
It melds hearts together, a bond to embolden,
A trust-giving elixir, in crystal flasks golden.

Translucent and shiny, it glimmers with truth,
The essence of promises, not fleeting as youth.
A sip between souls, an agreement unspoken,
A trust never shattered, nor ever broken.

Guard well this potion, with care and with love,
For trust is a treasure from the heavens above.
A tonic so rare, in the world's vast expanse,
In its luminescent presence, even lost hearts dance.

It heals the wounded, in quiet it speaks,
Filling the voids, and strengthening the weaks.
Hold fast to the tonic, with it never part,
For trust is the tincture that mends every heart.

## Blissful Blend of Being

A harmonious melody of feelings within,
Soothing and gentle, like a violin.
A blend of joy, peace, contentment combined,
In the cup of existence, so perfectly designed.

Breath of the calm breeze, whisper of the stream,
Caress of sun's rays, like a soft daydream.
In this blend, the heart finds its charming chant,
The soul's sweet symphony, no element scant.

Through lush fields of serenity it flows,
A gentle embrace in life's ebbs and its throes.
Drinking deeply from this tranquil brew,
Life's vivid colors come into view.

Every sip a story of love and grace,
Each drop a moment in the perfect place.
Blissful blend of being, forever to savor,
Life's myriad tastes, for us to favor.

## Lover's Lane Liquor

Infused with the giggles of shy, early love,
A dash of blush and stardust from above.
Lover's lane liquor, sweet and divine,
Fills the spirit with warmth, like summer's fine wine.

Whispers of romance in every glass,
Future, present entwined, and echoes of past.
Each sip a sonnet, each gulp a song,
Where two hearts converge, where they truly belong.

With every draught, the world starts to spin,
Revolving around a lover's sweet grin.
Intoxicating passion, a rhapsodic elixir,
More potent than moonlight, than stars it glitters.

Savor the essence of affection so dear,
In this lover's lane liquor, there's nothing to fear.
The dance of devotion, the rhythm of hearts,
When the liquor is poured, the magic starts.

## Heart's Hallowed Liquid

Flowing through veins like a mystical river,
A liquid love potion, a ceaseless giver.
Heart's hallowed liquid, it ebbs and it flows,
A fountain of feelings that every heart knows.

In this sacred draught, there's solace and pain,
Elation so bright, and sorrow's refrain.
It's the essence of life in an endless cascade,
In every beat echoed, its worth is displayed.

The pulse of existence, the heartbeat of time,
In every drawn breath, a reason, a rhyme.
The essence of essence, fluid and free,
Coursing through channels where it wishes to be.

Precious and priceless, a nectar so pure,
Through trials and tribulations, it finds the cure.
Heart's hallowed liquid, an unspoken pact,
In the sanctity of love, it's the final act.

www.ingramcontent.com/pod-product-compliance
Lightning Source LLC
La Vergne TN
LVHW020422070526
838199LV00003B/236

* 9 7 8 9 9 1 6 3 9 4 4 7 2 *